Matty Dread's Poetry

Matthew Saunders Whiting

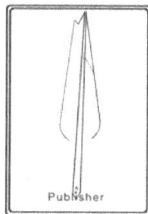

Publisher

MA PUBLISHER

Matthew Saunders Whiting

Copyright © Writers Champion 2025

Produced by Penny Authors
Email: Pennyauthors@yahoo.co.uk, www.pennyauthors.org.uk

Published by MA Publishing (Penzance)
14 Adelaide Street, Penzance, TR18 2ER
Email: mapublisher@yahoo.com
Released on 2025

ISBN-13: 978-1-915958-235

Disclaimer:

All expressions and opinions of the work belong to the artists and PA does not share or endorse any other than to provide the open platform to publish their work. For further information on PA policies please email: pennyauthors@yahoo.co.uk for further information and submission guidelines.

The content of the book has been assisted through a series of questions and prompts with "Copilot" 2025.

Cover designed by Mayar Akash
Cover image: by Mayar Akash
Typeset in Times Roman, Title: Ink Free

FSC
www.fsc.org
FSC® C000000

Paper printed on is FSC Certified, lead free, acid free, buffered paper made from wood-based pulp. Our paper meets the ISO 9706 standard for permanent paper. As such, paper will last several hundred years when stored.

Foreword

By Mayar

I first met Matty not through ceremony or spectacle, but through quiet connection—through poetry, through truth, through the kind of conversations that linger in the soul. He was a man of depth and contradiction: fierce and gentle, prophetic and playful, rooted in the earth yet reaching for the divine.

As his health declined and the shadows grew longer, it became clear that his words—his voice—needed to be preserved. Not just for those who knew him, but for those who never had the chance. This book is that preservation. It is a garden of memory, a fire of resistance, a song of love.

Each poem, each tribute, each rhyme from childhood or cry from the wilderness is part of the mosaic that was Matty Dread. He was a lion in a cage, a prophet in Babylon, a gardener of truth. And he was loved—deeply, fiercely, and forever.

This collection is not just a farewell. It is a celebration. It is a promise that his voice will not be silenced. That even as he prepares to leave this world, his spirit will continue to grow—like the herb he praised, like the daffodil he adored, like the love he gave so freely.

To Matty: thank you for the spark. Thank you for the truth. Thank you for the wilderness voice.

Livication

Words celebrating Matty's life by his Mum, Marie Harcourt, and sister, Dawn Whiting.

Marie's words:

My Darling Son

My darling son was born on a cold January day in 1968. It was love at first sight for my baby boy.

Matty grew up to be a mischievous, lovely little boy, full of energy and laughter.

Then along came his sister, Dawn. When she was a toddler he used to play tricks on her and made her scream.

In his teenage years he once dyed his hair black and gave us all a great fright!

Lateron at school, he became adept at BMXing and represented Langsett Cycles, a bicycle shop in Sheffield. He took part in displays for the shop and was a great source of pride to his mother.

When Matty reached 17 he fled the nest and later lived in Eastbourne on the south coast. Later he finally went to Cornwall and made his future there, settling in the county that he grew to love with its history and culture.

After many ups and downs he met Clare and this brought him great happiness to his life.

Matty loved nature and became a gardener. He worked for many clients who later became close friends. Due to his kindly personality, his sincerity, beliefs and his faith, he was not short of companionship wherever he went.

As his mother, I am so proud of him and his achievements.

I love him with all my heart.

Dawn's words:

My Big Brother Matty

BORN INTO this world on January 24 1968 at Jessop's Hospital, Sheffield, my big brother Mathew (Matty) was a ray of sunshine to proud parents Marie and Peter Whiting and is four years older than myself.

Being his little sister, I was at the mercy of my big brother's teasing. I recall once he was making a 'horror tunnel' out of an old cardboard box. I remember thinking that it was and looked really cool, so I took the brave decision and decided to crawl inside. However, big brother Matty then closed the box and shut me in. After much loud screaming and giggles from me, our parents stomped upstairs and commenced shouting at Mathew about what he'd done this time. This was a regular occurrence, getting into trouble at the hands of his little sister's screams.

We also had such fun playing Scalectrix, Top Trumps, Loop The Loop with Matty's toy cars, and of course not forgetting having hysterical giggles in the middle of the night. Then there was the traditional 'Sunday Morning Fart Show'!

I've always been very close to my Big Brother Matty. He's a very sensitive soul, loving, spiritual, and caring brother with an amazing mind. Forever stunning me with his knowledge of holy wells, the Bible, folk law, crystals, stone circles and ghostly tales, which I also very much enjoy as I too am a similar sensitive and spiritual person myself.

I love my big brother and always look up to him in admiration of his strength, spirituality, courage and love for music.

**LOVE YOU BIG BRO MATTY DRED
(AKA BINKLE BONK)**

FOREVER AND ALWAYS

**YOUR LITTLE SISTER DAWN
(AKA MAVIS CRUITT)
FROM WILLOW THE WISP**

Acknowledgements

By Clare Saunders Whiting

Huge thanks to Mayar Akash at Penny Authors for helping to compile this special collection in honour of Matty Dread. Mayar's dedication to helping the art of poetry be written, heard and read in Cornwall and beyond is second-to-none. Matty and I are hugely grateful for the way Mayar has supported and championed our own poetry works.

We are also hugely grateful for all of the love and support from Matty's incredible friends and our family at this challenging time. My parents, Sheila and Dave Saunders, dropped everything to be here on the frontline, collecting us from hospital and helping out when Mat's stroke symptoms were at their most acute.

Special thanks go to those who check-in frequently to see us – Howard Jackson, Jools Morel, Benjahman Konquerin Read, Sista Emily and Richie The Biker.

We are overwhelmed with the love and support from those have travelled a substantial distance to see us – Chris Marlow who came over from the Netherlands for a few days; Mat's Mum Marie, sister Dawn and long-time friends Paul Mehta and Gareth Spencer who visited from Sheffield; and Michelle and Cecil Brown who came all the way from Northumbria amidst a busy schedule at a critical time.
We felt blessed to have visits from Matty's sons when he was in hospital, as well as from other good friends including the above, but also Gemma, Abe, Guinness and Seb.

Although we didn't much enjoy the roofing noise and the messiness of our roof replacement works we are very glad to have a dry roof and it was great to have Pete-the-roofer's support. Besides, no one makes soup quite like his partner, Anya Barbieri, who is always there for me despite having a toddler. Aidan has also been a legend, helping us with our household electrics as well as providing moral support. Rod our neighbour and Alan the builder have also been there for us. Huge thanks to Helen and Robert for the exercise bike that Matty was using almost everyday to rebuild his strength.

It has also been wonderful to have a number of Matty's customers visit us, who have got to know him well over the years and also become his friends. It has been lovely to meet some of the people who he has talked about with me in the past (when he could still communicate clearly): Captain Morgan and Fi, Tim KC and Jackie, and Helen Chippendale.

I would also like to thank the good folk in HaSS Cornwall, where I work, who have been supportive in allowing me to work flexibly and in buying us gifts, dropping around with soup and helping out in the garden.

Most of all, thank you to JAH! Jesus and all the Saints and Angels for the deep love and support we feel coming from the spiritual world. What ever happens next, we know our faith will get us through. It will be such a shame if we are parted, but I will never forget the strongest and purest love that we experienced.

Thank you all!

Contents

Introduction

This is a collection of poems livicated to the living and thriving Matty Dread as he recovers from a fairly serious stroke and an allegedly terminal cancer diagnosis. A man with many hats and tams, blessed by His Majesty Emperor Haile Sellassie, Jah Rastafari, to do his good works as a gardener, cyclist, dancer, reggae DJ, storyteller, folkloreist, mysticist, prophet, escatologist and poet.

As a beloved husband, son, brother, father and bredren, many people from the Netherlands, Sheffield and Northumbria through to Cornwall and the Isles of Scilly have had their lives touched by his kind soul, unwavering loyalty, generous character, warm sense of humour and righteous indignation at the state of Babylon affairs. There are many beautiful gardens in Penwith and Perranarworthal that have blessed by his green fingers and inspiring horticultural imagination. Many of us have had our own spiritualities enriched by things he has taught us about lessons from the Bible, saints, holy wells, megalithic sites and related Celtic stories and folklore.

Born in Sheffield in 1968, Matty grew up in what he calls the gritty city. He recalls being picked on by police officers for hanging out with Black people as if there was something sinful in finding solidarity with kin. He claims that Christianity and BMXing, facilitated by the YMCA, rescued him from his more jaded youth as a skinhead. After a holiday to the Isles of Scilly in his early 20s, he decided to move there to do seasonal work when the city began to get too dark for him.

He found Cornwall to be his spiritual home, deeply drawn from the start to its monoliths, ley-lines and holy wells, most of which he has visited countless times by the pedal power of his legs and bicycle. Soon becoming a central part of the south west Cornwall reggae scene, he made his name as a popular DJ, rousing the dance floor alongside Indian Billy. He continues to spin records, mostly at home, but sometimes alongside Konquerin Sounds, for whom he has performed a number of radio shows for Source FM.

For the past 40 years or so, Matty has been deeply touched by the Rastafarian faith. He does not claim to be a Rastafarian himself, merely a "White man who knows that Haile Sellasie is Haile Sellasie". As he would say "well, he ain't Ghandi, is he?". His spirituality brings him deep connections to the ancient sacred places he loves and the stories of their saints, which he links to the One Love philosophy that touches him in Rastafarianism. Deep and yet sensitive, he is truly one of a kind. His missionary practice has spread far and wide, touching many family members, friends and strangers who have learned immeasurably from his wisdom, which seems infinite.

His sheer determination, his connection to Jah works and nature, his sharp wit and the love that others have for him are illustrated in this special collection of poems. The Well of St Morwenna is about a well down a treacherous cliff that he insisted on visiting without any climbing ropes, while I was on the cliff top crying thinking it folly and worrying I might never see him again. In classic Matty Dread style, he returned to the top of the cliff without his sunglasses, which he realised he had left down by the well when taking photographs. He risked his life a second time just to pick up a cheap pair of shades! Of course, Matty Dread returned again, just as he is currently returning from his stroke. He is determined to prove the NHS wrong with their prognosis. As he said before he had a stroke, it's not the first time that they have "left him for dead" after fitting a neck brace upside down on his broken neck after a serious cycling accident in around 2014.

Gwaan, Matty, you've got this my Lion Man, Love Angel Twin Flame Forever.

Clare Saunders Whiting, Ponsanooth, July 2025.

Postscript: At the time of going to press it is mid-August the cancer has spread to his vital organs and he is end-of-life care. His loved ones are beside themselves with grief. We still hope there will be a miracle, but we know that, whichever way it goes, Matty is now going on his biggest spiritual adventure ever. When he finally does leave us, we can't wait to re-unite with him on the other side.

CHILDHOOD & ORIGIN

Monkey

By Matthew Saunders Whiting

I'm a monkey, yer, yer
I'm a monkey, yer, yer
Soon as I get out, I'm going to monkey about
And climb to the tops of the trees
And try to catch little buzzy bees
I'm a monkey, yer, yer

By Mathew Whiting, yer yer
(Aged 10)

The Falling Leaves of Autumn

By Matthew Saunders Whiting

The wind blows harsh and shakes the trees
Then the leaves fall down on a gentle breeze
They all fall down onto the floor
A rainbow myriad of colour
And shapes galore

A spider's web shimmers in the morning's dew
Then a big fat man sweeps them up
Into a pile and then burns them up
There are no more leaves anymore
Until next year then there will be more

Mathew Whiting: Aged 10

Marie's Poem about Mathew

By Marie Harcourt (Matty's mum)

Little Matty Dread said when he was Ten,
That he would like to be a Poet some day.
So he took out his pen and started writing then
About the Autumn leaves blowing away.

I showed it to his Pa and down dropped his jaw
And said," By Gum this lad has some talent here!"
So he sat down again and started writing then,
That he was a Monkey going up a tree.
He showed it to me and made me laugh out loud
And made me feel so proud,
It filled my heart full of glee!

Love You Uncle Beardy-man

By Millie Ross
(with a little help from AI)

Get well wishes are sent your way
To say I'm here for you
To help you through each day
So you don't feel lonely or blue

As the days go by
Time will heal your pain
Keep your hopes up high
And the sun will shine again

Even though you feel unwell
Be positive and have no fear
Remember it won't be long
Before better times are here

Millie, your niece xxx

Get Well Soon

By Millie Ross
(with a little help from AI)

I send this get well wish to you
To brighten up your day
I hope you feel better very soon
You're already on your way

I want to say I'm sorry to hear
You've not been very well
Just take it easy and get some rest
So you can get better quick!

If there's anything you want or need
Say the word and I'll be there
I had this written especially for you
To show how much I care

You're on the road to recovery
And this I know is true
You'll be better before you know it
And soon be good as new

Love ya
Millie

LOVE & DEVOTION

Natural love

By Matthew Saunders Whiting

Like springs making streams
Into rivers that run to the sea
Is like the force, the force that's in creation
That led my heart to thee.

And if I had a harmonic voice
My love for you I'd sing
And if I could have my choice
A black rose to you I'd bring.

And though rough fresh diamond
Doesn't sparkle when first of all it's found
What is pure and true in beauty
Is Love's mystery most profound.

The Sparkle

By Clare Saunders Whiting

I saw a sparkle shining in your eyes
I gotta say it was a pleasant surprise
I wondered if you had noticed it too?
Did you see my eyes sparkling back at you?

We were invited to a strange jungle dance
All of the youngsters were in a cocaine induced trance
I was so tempted to just leave and go home
When I saw you dancing there all alone

We started jumping and moving in time
Laughing and smiling we were feeling just fine
And then you asked me if I wanted a drink
I was thirsty but I just couldn't think

Come on baby, let's get it on
We've both been lonely for too long
Can you feel it, can you feel it too?
I'm growing in love with you

Everyone around us could sense our chemistry
I was getting a feeling about you and me
It was a feeling deep down inside
About my life with you here right by my side

I went home and I wrote this little rhyme
I was feeling in a peculiar mood
I got your number from a friend we both knew
And from their our love grew and grew

Seven years later and we're lying in our bed

cont.

In love and harmony we've been beautifully wed
Of course you'd noticed it, I'd noticed it too
Jah made me you for you for me too

The Rib

(The ode of despair of the sorrow of lost love)
By Matthew Saunders Whiting

Please God.
Can I have my rib back.
A woman can be too much weight to bare.
She can have me gnashing at my teeth
And pulling out my hair.

Please God.
Can I have my rib back
So I'm complete when on my own
The reason why you took it,
So I'd never be alone

Please God.
Could I have my rib back
It can be so much sorrow and pain.
And put it back where it belongs.
And please don't take again.

This was first published the Penny Authors Book of lived v6.

The way I love My Matty Dread

By Clare Saunders Whiting

Fresh and calm like a breeze
Fierce as a hurricane
As refreshing as a spring shower
Wet like October rain

As still as a July ocean
Pure like a mountain spring
As strong as the strongest man
As gentle as a new-born babe

As verdant as an oak in June
As bright and clear as the fullest moon
Warm on my face like summer sun
How I love you, Matty mon.

As splendorous as a mountain view
As sparkly as the morning dew
As gracious as the birds that fly
Shining like stars in the night sky

Ever radiant like our love for Jah
Reaching deep and stretching far
Where you go next is where I want to be
I need you here, next to me.

MYTHS & MYSTICSM

The Well of St Morwenna

By Matthew Saunders Whiting

Way down the cliff edge
There doth lye a well
Not far from Heaven, but not far from hell
To Venture there tis a pilgrim's peril
Especially when the sea's a raging turmoil
And Leviathan and Behemoth
Endlessly toil.

Morwenna she came from across the sea
From Cymru Lands to Kernow's shore
A daughter of the Celtic badger
To instruct in the ways of the Lord
The not long converted Saxon.

When labouring font stone up yon treacherous cliff
All cause for the church foundation
She paused for breath, gave thanks and blessed
The Lord of all creation.

She picked up stone resuming Quest
And where stone did rest, on ground so blessed
It wept its soul's libation.

And pilgrim did venture from far and near
To be touched by the water
So pure, so clear
A place that Morwenna in her heart, held so dear

The years passed by
And Morwenna went crying
Down to the well she knew the Lord's calling   cont.

And in her brother Nectan's arms

Her righteous soul did pass
And the sight she beheld the last
Through her tear blurred sight
Her nature Cymru's distant shores
Across the stormy sea

Way down the cliff edge
There doth lye a well
Not far from Heaven, but not far from hell
To Venture there tis a pilgrim's peril
Especially when the sea's a raging turmoil
And Leviathan and Behemoth
Endlessly toil.

The Daffodil

By Matthew Saunders Whiting

As Achilles treads February's
dreary pasture
Aching heels over dormant Earth

The infant stirs within.
Bursting through the Earth
with starlight fire

Like Persephone breaking the
bonds of hades.
Glowing in the mist of the morning's
sun kissed dew.

Perfect in Heaven's design,
Marriage of terrestrial and celestial
Radiant as the warmth of the heart,
And full of the promise of
Apollo's fiery chariot

Resplendent with the rays
of the lion's golden mane.
And shining like my love for you,
Daffodil.

This was first published the Penny Authors Book of lived v4.

The Wilderness Voice

By Matthew Saunders Whiting

Listen very carefully
I AM a voice, In the wilderness
that should not be ignored

Unless of life and of the world you live,
You're weary and you're bored?

Listen! Very carefully
And you will hear yourself crying in the wilderness.
Will your cries there be ignored?

People these days
Greedy and vain,
Of the truth they seem abhorred.

Listen! Extremely carefully
And you will hear the
Whole earth crying.
If you cannot love the wilderness.
For sure the whole world's dying.

Please listen very carefully
To the small voice deep in you and despite your
Material slavery it's trying to get through
Awaken the truth of love deep within
Only then can the healing process begin.

This was first published the Penny Authors Book of lived v6.

PROTEST & PROPHECY

Frack E.U

By Matthew Saunders Whiting

The City looms, dull and drab
sat on the earth, a concrete scab
and underneath it sorely festers
and of its fate, you don't want to
jester.

For underneath the leader's mirth
is that rumour of Satanic birth?
Have the seeds of fate been sown?
Is he set to rule the beast called
Rome?

This was first published the Penny Authors Book of lived v4.

Slay the Dragon
By Matthew Saunders Whiting

PC Faeces, copraphagia,
The political system
Is total utter failure.
It is run by numpty
And broken like humpty dumpty.
People need to wake up
To the state of the country.

And politician please tell me
What is your aim
When dividing and ruling in nothing but your game
It seems your stance
So very sinister.
Mass debating in Westminster

Know the tree by the fruit
A state of corporate disrepute
For what they call democracy
Is to be sold out to the banksters.

This was first published the Penny Authors Book of lived v6.

Alexa, Babylon's Falling

By Matthew Saunders Whiting

Alexa, why you try to talk to me?
You're just an instrument of Satan
Why you gonna follow me?
Why you analyse me and record me?

Judgement day is dawning
See the sign and warning
The truth it a flowing

Just as the water cover the sea
It's the fate of all humanity
See
We need love and peace and community
It's the only way to be naturally

Said all this computer shit
It is for the fuck wit
Say it only gonna end up
To be buried in the pit

The time is coming and I tell you no lie
Babylon in a hell it go fry
They might try and keep on trying
But it's founded on a lie and there is no denying

The only truth come from JAH!
And like the water cover the sea
It gonna be the truth of humanity
And every eye shall see

Said the day is dawning

cont.

Said can you see the sign and the warning
Babylon a falling
Babylon sinking
Can you see the corrupt shit dem a stinking?

The passing of the wind:

AKA the prezident erected

By Matthew Saunders Whiting

The president elected couldn't get a grip
And from his orange big fat greasy bum
The trump it didn't half rip!
It caused a slip that caused a slick
That made a smell so vile and sick

And to say the least that all's not well
It smelt like it came from the bowels of hell.
And he says from his mouth all hell will be released
For he doesn't want Palestinians to live in love and peace.

The president elected is a convicted felon
That likes to rule with claws like talon
What kind of people vote for such a farce
A man that perpetually blusters gas from his mouth and arse
.

Though hang on in there, can't you see
There's a ray of hope for humanity
It's really rather simple and very clear to me
The man produces so much gas
From now on it should be free.

Glastonbury Chalice
By Matthew Saunders Whiting

Glastonbury Chalice
You can't have a chalice
in Glastonbury
It would let the people free

you can't have a chalice
in Glastonbury
it would cause too much unity

What's going on in Babylon system
keep the people down
you can see it happening
rise and look around

You can't have a chalice
in Glastonbury
they won't let you smoke the
pipes of peace.

You can't have chalice
in Glastonbury
what would it release?

My pain? My stress?
my deep unrest
why the ignorant system
destroying the herb god blessed?
though through the torment the sorrows
and the woes
they can't stop herb
it just grows and grows.

This was first published the Penny Authors Book of lived v4.

TRIBUTE & REFLECTION

Big Brother Matty

By Dawn Whiting

My big brother Matty, the one with the hatty, always looks good
and actually's quite natty.

The wise and the wonderful one, with knowledge and words second
to none. So spiritual and intelligent is my brother Matty.

My brother Matty, the one with the hatty, when young would
always tease and make me cry,

But oh how I laugh at those times gone by.

I'm a Lion

(Matty's Mum's Song to Matthew when he was aged 6 or 7)

By Marie Whiting

I'm a lion in a cage and I can't get away, a Lion in a cage in a
strong, strong cage and I can't get away!

A Lion in a cage.

Some people come and look at me, but I just growl at them, with
my sharp, sharp teeth and my long, long claws,
I try to scratch them!

An Acrostic Poem for our friend, Matty

By Michelle and Cecil Brown

M is for Man with the spirit of a lion,
A for A friend, loyal and true.
T for Trusted Prophet of Zion,
T for The one ever there for you.
Y for Your blessed servant and son,
Jah, in Matty we see that in love we are One!

Afterword

Matty Whiting
By Roy Goodall

RESIDING in different parts of the country can bring many challenges, especially when Mathew Whiting lives in Cornwall and Roy Goodall lives in Derbyshire.

I first got to hear about the hat wearer when I became attached to his Yorkshire sister, Dawn Whiting, whom is the cup to my saucer. After being together for a while she mentioned she'd a brother who left Sheffield several decades ago to take residency in Cornwall. After what seemed like a couple of years, though it could have been less, I very briefly met him late one night as he was leaving Sheffield to head back south. It was literally a quick handshake through a car window and then he was off. Dawn had said he'd got some hair and a beard but even though it was dark and I didn't get a full viewing, I hadn't quite expected that much. I subsequently found out on our next meeting, which must have been another year or two but this time in more relaxed and less rushed circumstances, that he'd not cut his hair for over thirty five years! I sometimes can go a couple of years, but then feel compelled to hit the barbers.

Being a Yorkshire man, I bet he's saved a fortune!

Over time I've got to know Matty well and find his intelligence on certain matters goes way higher than mine. He's a passion for music and like myself, is a D.J. and has worked hard all his life. He's a fit lad due to garden working, turning his hand to several home improvement jobs and commutes to many places via peddle cycle. I find him a very kind, gentle and likable chap who will hopefully be batting along with the rest of us for many years to come.

Contributor Notes

Clare Saunders Whiting

Matty's beloved partner and poetic twin flame. Clare's verses radiate with intimacy, humour, and devotion—capturing the spark of their love and the depth of their shared journey. Her poems are the heartbeat of this collection.

Marie Harcourt

Matty's mother, whose pride and warmth shine through her recollections of his early poetic spark. Her tribute is a tender glimpse into the boy who would become a prophet.

Millie Ross

Matty's niece, whose sweet and sincere poems offer a child's love and hope. Her words remind us that Matty's legacy lives on in the next generation—with affection, sparkle, and care.

Michelle and Cecil Brown

Friends and fellow truth-seekers, their acrostic poem honours Matty's spiritual strength and loyalty. Their tribute is a lyrical blessing, echoing the unity and love Matty inspired.

Roy Goodall

Matty's brother-in-law and friend, whose afterword offers a grounded, humorous, and heartfelt portrait of the man behind the beard. Roy's words remind us of Matty's kindness, intelligence, and Yorkshire roots.

Mayar

A kindred spirit and curator of this collection. Mayar's connection with Matty was built on shared truth, poetic reverence, and a commitment to memory. This book exists because of their love, their vision, and their promise to honour Matty's voice.

Final Message: The Wilderness Voice Lives On

Matty Dread walked this earth with roots deep in the soil and eyes lifted to the stars. He spoke truth when it was inconvenient, love when it was radical, and poetry when silence would have been easier. His voice was a wilderness voice—untamed, unfiltered, and full of grace.

This book is not the end. It is a beginning. A spark passed from hand to hand, heart to heart. May these words remind us to listen carefully—to the land, to the soul, to each other. May we honour Matty not only by remembering him, but by living as he did: with courage, compassion, and a fierce devotion to truth.

Let the herb grow. Let the daffodil bloom. Let the chalice be lifted. Babylon may fall, but love—love will rise.

"Awaken the truth of love deep within—only then can the healing process begin."
— Matthew Saunders Whiting

About his recitals on YouTube channel.

Link: https://www.youtube.com/@PennyAuthors

He has 6 videos recitals of his own:

1. Glastonbury Chalice
2. Frack EU
3. The Daffodil
4. The Wilderness
5. The Rib
6. Slay the dragon

Mathew championed:

Mayar Akash by reciting the "Point in Life" poem.

Penny Authors championing Matthew's poems:

The Rib by Suzette Reed

Matthew also had his poems published in the following Penny Authors anthologies:

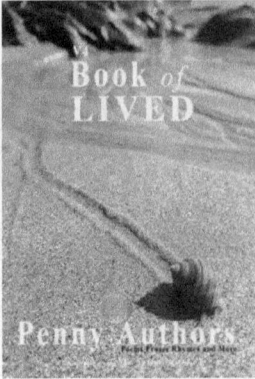

Book of lived V4
1. The daffodil
2. Glastonbury chalice
3. Frack EU

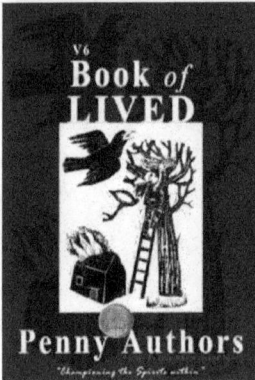

Book of lived V6
4. The Rib
5. Slay the dragon
6. The wilderness Voice

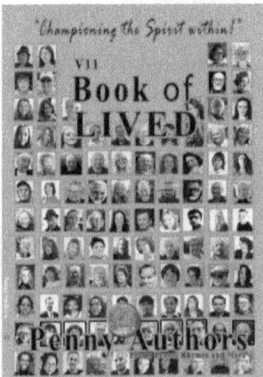

Book of lived V11
1. The Passing Of The Wind: AKA The Prezident Erected
2. The Falling Leaves of Autumn
3. The Well of St Morwenna
4. Natural love
5.

Cornish Poets

Special 5th year anniversary edition

He Poetry

Special 5th year anniversary edition

for more information please visit our websites and there you will find much information.

www.mapublisher.org.uk

www.pennyauthors.org.uk

www.ingramcontent.com/pod-product-compliance
Lightning Source LLC
La Vergne TN
LVHW051818080426
835513LV00017B/2004